Eleven
Vocabulary for 11 plus and CEM

INTRODUCTION

Vocabulary for 11 plus Book

This book is dedicated to all kids and their parents who are working hard to achieve good place in the grammar school. The book has words which need to be learned and practice, which are later used in cloze or other forms of writing.

Parents should use this book for helping kids to develop understanding and meaning of words.

Practice words which will help kids in doing cloze, verbal reasoning comprehension as well as good short and long writing.

This book includes words used in previous CEM exams.

Regards

S Brains

TABLE OF CONTENTS

WORDS SET 1

Abandon - leave

Amend - improve

Authorize - permit

Activate - start

Adamant - stubborn

Brave - courageous

Box - carton

Bind - join

Brilliant - shiny

Bear - panda

Creature - animal

Climb - ascend

1

Correct - right

Charmed - enchanted

Contract - shrink

Cautious - careful

Courteous - polite

Deficiency - shortage

Deliberately - purposely

Drizzle - rain

Delicate - fragile

Dilemma - predicament

Demolish - destroy

Disperse - scatter

Dessert - sweet

Enough - adequate

Eliminate - destroy

Edible - eatable

Equal - divide

Expand - elevate

Expensive - dear

Exhausted - weary

Frequent - often

Freak - abnormal

Flat - apartment

Frank - blunt

Ghost - spectre

Glum - gloomy

Hostile - unfriendly

Halt - stop

Hesitate - delay

Implore - beg

Incredible - unbelievable

Interior - inside

Invented - imaginary

Jump - leap

Just - fair

Join - combine

Keyboard – strings

Kneel - chime

Lure - attract

Mere - bare

Mumble - murmur

Misfortune - adversity

Mammoth - huge

Minimum - least

Moist - damp

Motive - purpose

Modest - humble

Munch - chew

Nimble – agile, quick thinking

Neglect - ignore

Oral - verbal

Orbit - path

Pant - gasp

Persuade - convince

Penalty - punishment

Purchase - buy

✓ Package - parcel

Perplex- puzzle

✓ Quiet - serene

Rule - govern

Revolt - riot

✓ Refugee - outlaw

✓ Rabbit - hare

✓ Receive - accept

Stone - rock

Shimmer - shine

Slip – fail to make grip

✓ Skate - slide

Slide - skid

✓ Similar - alike

Spite – malice, desire to hurt

Stop - halt

Sadness - pity

Shiver - tremble

Seal – fasten

Scarce - rare

Tame - gentle

Tug - pull

Tremble - quake

Tepid -warm

Unwilling - reluctant

Under - beneath

Velocity - speed

Vanquish - conquer

Valiant- brave

Watch - look

Walk - stroll

Wonder – question

Yell - shout

Yield - submit

VOCABULARY TEST FOR SET 1

1. the land ___ grapes and tobacco:

    a) yields

    b) commotion

    c) scurry

    d) zeal

2. He successfully ____ the rival king.

    a) aplomb

    b) Vanquish

    c) yields

    d) tactic

3. reluctant is the similar of:

    a) agitated

    b) Unwilling

    c) uneasy

    d) relaxed

4. he soaked a flannel in the _____ water

   a) bored

   b) engrossed

   c) tepid

   d) unfocused

5. tens of thousands of _____ fled their homes

   a) accepted

   b) refugees

   c) expelled

   d) inducted

6. they _____ in the damp foggy cold

   a) traffic

   b) shivered

   c) route

   d) way

7. the front wheels began to ___

   a) bluffing

   b) slip

   c) commotion

   d) recuperate

8. synonyms of rebel:

   a) brackish

   b) revolt

   c) friendly

   d) happy

9. The army was requested to ___ the war

   a) brandishing

   b) cutting

   c) halt

   d) painting

10. The wheel's ＿＿ due to overloaded wagon.

  a) circumference

  b) Trembled

  c) firmness

  d) tightness

11. The elephant is also called ＿＿.

  a) cunning

  b) shy

  c) lazy

  d) Mammoth

12. There was ＿＿ point on team after a fight broke in between the match.

  a) construction

  b) Penalty

  c) debris

  d) order

13. The people were _____ to the failing government.

    a) according

    b) Courteous

    c) imaginative

    d) courage

14. People marveled at the skillfulness of her fingers as she played the _____.

    a) keyboard

    b) pen

    c) writing

    d) deftness

15. Synonyms of attract.

    a) engross

    b) Lure

    c) Neglect

    d) dread

16. You should be _____ about crimes in your area.

   a) boring

   b) simple

   c) petty

   d) Cautious

17. a dread of _____ and witches affected every aspect of daily life .

   a) embers

   b) driftwood

   c) spectres

   d) kindling

18. She was so ___ that she didn't notice her teacher enter the room.

   a) entertained

   b) Oral

   c) engrossed

   d) tired

19. he was _____ when he reached the top from the mist.

   a) panting

   b) became

   c) blew

   d) emerged

20. puzzle also means:

   a) annoyance

   b) perplex

   c) calmness

   d) relaxation

21. He is _____ that he is not going to resign.

   a) noisy

   b) tiring

   c) adamant

   d) exhilarating

22. Valiant also means:

    a) brave

    b) taste

    c) appearance

    d) softness

23. Do ___ if you need extra paper during exams.

    a) funny

    b) Yell

    c) crazy

    d) angry

24. The Tug is the similar of

    a) easy

    b) effortless

    c) pull

    d) grueling

25. He put the house up for sale to _____ his family.

    a) gusto

    b) dread

    c) spite

    d) apprehension

26. The teacher says the student behavior was a total _____.

    a) paperwork

    b) freak

    c) headway

    d) ashamed

27. Synonyms of agile

    a) ignited

    b) Nimble

    c) ignored

    d) cheated

28. Synonyms of stroll

    a) confused

    b) lay

    c) walk

    d) play

29. The shrub has small _____berries.

    a) edible

    b) waste

    c) substantial

    d) apprehensive

30. The king was____ and people like him a lot.

    a) ungrateful

    b) Modest

    c) imperious

    d) shy

WORDS SET 2

Abundance – surplus, plentiful

Alert - vigilant

Benefit – good, sake

Beck - stream

Clemency – mercy, lenience

Conclusion – finish

Debrief - question

Deliberate - intentional

Emerge - appear

Evaluation - assessment

Flamboyant - confident

Frivolous - light-hearted

Gregarious - social

Grotesque – deformed

Helix - spiral

Humble - meek, helpful

Inaugural - first

Inaugurate - begin

Lavish - grand

Matte - dull

Nauseous - sick

Nurseryman - a person who owns or works in a place where plants are grown

Orthodontist - a specialist who has undergone special training in a dental school

Ostentatious - showy

VOCABULARY TEST FOR SET 2

1. The synonym of begin is:

    a. Invalid.

    b. Inaugurate.

    c. Prompt.

    d. Deliberate.

2. Humble means:

    a. Penalty.

    b. Inaugural.

    c. meek.

    d. Quality.

3. Abundance is similar to:

    a. Complain.

    b. Respect.

    c. Plenty.

    d. Conquer.

4. A synonym of Helix is:

    a. civil

    b. Spiral

    c. curve

    d. slow

5. The opposite of Alert is:

    a. careless

    b. careful

    c. tolerance

    d. valor

6. Grotesque also means:

    a. deformed

    b. complex

    c. delicate

    d. helix

7. The opposite meaning of the word Matte is:

    a. believer

    b. bright

    c. dull

    d. pale

8. The opposite term for Deliberate is:

    a. imaginary

    b. heedless

    c. actual

    d. critical

9. lenience is the similar word for:

    a. Clemency

    b. digress

    c. diminish

    d. improve

10. The word with the same meaning as Frivolous is:

    a. deplete

    b. handle

    c. simplify

    d. silly

11. The similar word for Evaluation is:

    a. obedient

    b. decision

    c. objectionable

    d. biased

12. The word Debrief is the opposite for:

    a. question

    b. answer

    c. tempt

    d. laconic

13. The word with the same meaning confident as is:

    a. Evaluation

    b. Flamboyant

    c. Debrief

    d. cheerful

14. Ostentatious means the same as:

    a. medium

    b. showy

    c. sufficient

    d. proficient

15. Lavish is the opposite word for:

    a. diverse

    b. dismiss

    c. grand

    d. demines

WORDS SET 3

Adversary - opponent

Aplomb - calm

Apprehensive - worried

Aptitude - ability

Attentive - engrossed

Banish - expel

Barricade - barrier

Bluff - pretend

Brackish - salty

Brandish - wave

Circumference - border

Commotion - disruption

Concoction - mixture

Conspicuous - eye-catching

Contortion - deformation

Counter - reply

Cunning - sly

Debris - rubble

Defiance - rebelliousness

Deft - skillful

Destination - goal

Diminish - lessen

Disdain - scorn

Dispel - drive away

Dismal - depressing

Eavesdrop - listen in (without permission)

Egregious - reprehensible

Ember - coal

Emerge - appear

Engross - immerse

Exasperation - annoyance

Exhilarate - thrill

Falter - hesitate

Foresight - see or know ahead

Fragrance - scent

Furtive - sneaky

Grueling - laborious

Gusto - enthusiasm

Habitation - dwelling

Hasten - rush

Headway - progress

Ignite - burn

Illuminate - clear up

Impending - imminent (near at hand or about to happen)

Imperious - arrogantly superior

Jabber - ranting

Jargon - slang

Jostle - shove

Jut - protrude

Kindle - inflame

Knoll - small mound or hill

Luminous - bright

Malleable - pliable

Materialize - happen

Meander - curve; bend

Meticulous - precise; exact

Misgiving - qualm; uneasy

Momentum - strong strength

Monotonous - flat; dull; unchanging

Multitude - several

Muster - gather

Narrate - tell; recite

Obscure - unclear

Ominous - threatening

Outlandish - bizarre; strange; unusual

Persistent - relentless

Pertinent - relevant

Plenteous - abundant

Potential - possible; likely

Precipice - cliff

Pristine - pure

Quell - stop; subdue

Recluse - hermit

Recuperate - recover; get well

Replenish - refill

Repugnant - offensive; repulsive

Restitution - compensation; amends

Sabotage - destroy

Scarcity - insufficiency

Scurry - scamper

Serenity - tranquility

Sociable - friendly

Somber - grave

Specimen - sample

Stamina - endurance

Subside - weaken

Swagger - style; gait

Swarm - drove

Tactic - maneuver

Terse - curt

Translucent - clear

Uncanny - extraordinary

Unsightly - ugly

Versatile - variable

Vigilant - watchful

Vulnerable - defenseless

Waft - drift

Waver - hesitate

Weather - endure

Zeal - eagerness

VOCABULARY TEST FOR SET 3

1. When people are arguing over something, they are called:

   a) adversaries

   b) commotion

   c) scurry

   d) zeal

2. He was ____ when he heard the news.

   a) aplomb

   b) pristine

   c) serenity

   d) tactic

3. Apprehensive is the opposite of:

   a) agitated

   b) worried

   c) uneasy

   d) relaxed

4. A person who is attentive is someone who is

   a) bored

   b) engrossed

   c) disinterested

   d) unfocused

5. Anna was banished from her club.
   That means she was:

   a) accepted

   b) branded

   c) expelled

   d) inducted

6. A roadblock is also called a :

   a) traffic

   b) barrier

   c) route

   d) way

7. Poker players are great at :

   a) bluffing

   b) contortion

   c) commotion

   d) recuperate

8. There are lots of living things that dwell in slightly salty water, also called:

   a) brackish

   b) briny

   c) fresh

   d) diluted

9. The angry man is ___ a sword:

   a) brandishing

   b) cutting

   c) contorting

   d) painting

10. The wheel's _____ is too large for the wagon.

   a) circumference

   b) roundness

   c) firmness

   d) tightness

11. The fox is a/an ___ animal.

   a) cunning

   b) shy

   c) lazy

   d) endangered

12. There was so much _____ after a fire broke in the mall.

   a) construction

   b) new goods

   c) debris

   d) order

13. There was so much ____ in the people's eyes when they were fighting for their freedom against a tyrant government.

    a) arrogance

    b) defiance

    c) defeat

    d) discouragement

14. People marveled at the ___ of her fingers as she played the piano.

    a) stiffness

    b) clumsiness

    c) unskillful

    d) deftness

15. You shouldn't ____ on people.

    a) engross

    b) falter

    c) eavesdrop

    d) dread

16. It's chilling to hear about _____ crimes on the news.

   a) boring

   b) simple

   c) petty

   d) egregious

17. All that was left of the grand house was ___ after someone set fire on it.

   a) embers

   b) driftwood

   c) tinder

   d) kindling

18. She was so ___ in the novel that she didn't notice her teacher enter the room.

   a) entertained

   b) bored

   c) engrossed

   d) tired

19. It was a magical moment when the fairy ____ from the mist.

    a) vanished

    b) became

    c) blew

    d) emerged

20. Exasperation also means:

    a) annoyance

    b) excitement

    c) calmness

    d) relaxation

21. Riding roller coasters is a/an ____ experience.

    a) noisy

    b) tiring

    c) uninspiring

    d) exhilarating

22. Fragrance also means:

   a) scent

   b) taste

   c) appearance

   d) softness

23. Do not make any ___ glances on anyone else's paper during exams.

   a) funny

   b) furtive

   c) crazy

   d) angry

24. The Chemistry experiment was so complicated. It was a/ an ___task.

   a) easy

   b) effortless

   c) simple

   d) grueling

25. Aunt May baked Harry's favorite chocolate cake. He ate with such____.

    a) gusto

    b) dread

    c) grumbling

    d) apprehension

26. Finally, after pending a few hours in the library, Jenny is already making ____ with her homework.

    a) paperwork

    b) writing

    c) headway

    d) delay

27. Studying the nation's history ____ love for the country

    a) ignited

    b) made

    c) ignored

    d) created

28. After the teacher lectured about the American Civil War, the students were _____ about what freedom cost.

    a) confused

    b) unconcerned

    c) baffled

    d) illuminated

29. She was very nervous about the _____ release of the exam results, within the hour.

    a) consistent

    b) impending

    c) substantial

    d) apprehensive

30. The tyrant king was_____ and people did not like him a bit.

    a) ungrateful

    b) sordid

    c) imperious

    d) shy

31. Grant did not like hearing his friend ____ about his new car.

    a) jabber

    b) laugh

    c) write

    d) drive

32. Scientists often use ____ to explain ideas.

    a) jargon

    b) music

    c) poems

    d) lyrics

33. Jane takes a deep breath to ____ her strong emotions.

    a) improve

    b) ignore

    c) express

    d) quell

34. The old ___ lived alone in the woods.

    a) refuse

    b) excuse

    c) recluse

    d) misuse

35. My father spent 5 days in the hospital, _____ after an accident.

    a) working

    b) recuperating

    c) sleeping

    d) shopping

36. Please buy more office supplies to ____ our stock.

    a) remove

    b) use up

    c) destroy

    d) replenish

37. Her nasty habit is ___:

   a) repugnant.

   b) adorable.

   c) recognizable.

   d) Entertaining.

38. The judge ordered him to pay the victim for _____

   a) respect.

   b) punishment.

   c) restitution.

   d) payment.

39. His opponents stole his work and tried to ____ him.

   a) reward

   b) applaud

   c) praise

   d) sabotage

40. Famine is when there is ____ of food.

    a) plenty

    b) abundance

    c) overflowing

    d) scarcity

41. The squirrel started to _____ away after taking food from the picnic basket.

    a) sleep

    b) scurry

    c) dig

    d) sweep

42. The mountain lake was a place of _____.

    a) raucous.

    b) rage.

    c) serenity.

    d) party.

43. There was a _____ of ants on the picnic grounds.

   a) swarm

   b) group

   c) collection

   d) line

44. The cops were very _____ while they guarded the bank at night.

   a) lazy

   b) happy

   c) jubilant

   d) vigilant

45. Geniuses have ___ ways of solving problems.

   a) uncanny

   b) ineffective

   c) confusing

   d) uninspiring

46. Little children are ____ and must be protected.

   a) happy

   b) vulnerable

   c) excited

   d) sad

47. On a hot summer day, a ___ of cool air is very refreshing.

   a) waft

   b) drop

   c) smell

   d) sound

48. Do not ____ in your desire to reach your goals.

   a) stop

   b) rush

   c) waver

   d) ignore

49. She was a very inspiring person. She was able to ____ so many storms of life.

    a) weather

    b) give up

    c) run away from

    d) achieve

50. Students should show ____ in learning.

    a) boredom

    b) zeal

    c) disinterest

    d) laziness

WORDS SET 4

Rational - sound

Attribute - quality

Subdue - conquer

Animated - lively

Awe - reverence, wonder

Intricate - complex

Skeptic - doubter

Hypothetical - imaginary, supposed

Enhance - improve; improve

Manipulate - handle

Subjective - personal; prejudiced

Succinct - concise

Enthusiastic - eager

Adequate - sufficient

Uniform - consistent

Ecstatic - thrilled

Affect - influence

Wary - on guard; leery

Novel - new; original

Continuous - uninterrupted

Courtesy - civility

Fallacy - trickery

Frail - delicate

Subsequent - resultant

Nonchalant - casual; unconcerned

Hoax - ruse

Composure - poise

Excise - remove

Disperse - scatter

Eccentric - peculiar; odd

Commendable - admirable

Domain - territory

Passive - inactive

Liberate - release

Faltering - unsteady

Vast - immense

Comply - obey

Optimum - most desirable; best

Enlighten - teach

Tedious - tiresome

Exonerate - clear; acquit

Ephemeral - short-lived; transient; passing

Predecessor - forerunner; precursor

Refrain - desist, stop

Affable - amiable; friendly

Rigorous - strict

Orient - adjust; become familiar

Levitate - raise; lift

Oblivious - unmindful

Verify - confirm

Pacify - appease; placate

Plausible - believable

Idle - lazy

Avid - eager; greedy

Meek - tame; humble

Complacent - content

Ambiguous - equivocal; unclear

Confer - bestow; discuss

Repast - meal

Esteem - respect

Eloquent - eloquent; articulate

Apathetic - uninterested; indifferent

Deterrent - hindrance

Impertinent - rude

Augment - grow; increase

Ludicrous - absurd

Archaic - old; primitive

Incredulous- distrustful; disbelieving

Vindictive - revengeful; unforgiving

Sullen - gloomy

Menial - lowly; unskilled

Panacea - cure-all; remedy

Taut - tense

Rile - irritate

Glib - superficial and false words; insincere

Mar - defect; blemish

Cognizant - aware; conscious

Mediate - intercede

Concurrent - synchronous; simultaneous

Induce - stimulate; cause

Intrepid - dauntless; brave

Saturate - fill; soak

Methodical - organized

Latent - potential; inactive

Proscribe - prohibit

Prevarication - falseness

Mirth - glee; merriment

Surreptitious - sneaky

Trepidation - dread; apprehension

VOCABULARY TEST FOR SET 4

1. The synonym of rational is:

   a) invalid.

   b) sound.

   c) prompt.

   d) deliberate

2. Attribute means:

   a) penalty.

   b) admission.

   c) speech.

   d) quality.

3. Subdue is similar to:

   a) complain.

   b) respect.

   c) deny.

   d) conquer.

4. A synonym of animated is:

    a) civil

    b) lively

    c) abbreviated

    d) secret

5. The opposite of awe is:

    a) reverence

    b) distortion

    c) contempt

    d) valor

6. Intricate also means:

    a) costly

    b) complex

    c) delicate

    d) prim

7. The opposite meaning of the word skeptic is:

   a) believer

   b) friend

   c) innovator

   d) politician

8. The opposite term for hypothetical is:

   a) imaginary

   b) specific

   c) actual

   d) uncritical

9. enhance is the opposite word for:

   a) deprive

   b) digress

   c) diminish

   d) improve

10. The word with the same meaning as manipulate is:

    a) deplete

    b) handle

    c) simplify

    d) nurture

11. The opposite word for subjective is:

    a) obedient

    b) invective

    c) objectionable

    d) unbiased

12. The word succinct is the opposite for:

    a) verbose

    b) feeble

    c) distinct

    d) laconic

13. The word with the same meaning as enthusiastic is:

    a) available

    b) eager

    c) adamant

    d) cheerful

14. Adequate means the same as:

    a) mediocre

    b) average

    c) sufficient

    d) proficient

15. Uniform is the opposite word for:

    a) diverse

    b) dissembling

    c) slovenly

    d) bizarre

16. The synonym for the word ecstatic is:

    a) positive

    b) thrilled

    c) inconsistent

    d) wild

17. The word that also means affect is:

    a) sicken

    b) cause

    c) influence

    d) accomplish

18. Wary is the opposite of:

    a) worried

    b) leery

    c) careless

    d) alert

19. The opposite word for novel is:

    a) old

    b) suitable

    c) dangerous

    d) unsettled

20. The other meaning of the word continuous is:

    a) adjacent

    b) contiguous

    c) intermittent

    d) uninterrupted

21. The synonym for the word courtesy is:

    a) rudeness

    b) conviviality

    c) congruity

    d) civility

22. The opposite word for fallacy is:

    a) blessing

    b) fable

    c) truth

    d) weakness

23. The synonym for the word frail is:

    a) robust

    b) delicate

    c) adaptable

    d) vivid

24. The opposite meaning of subsequent is:

    a) previous

    b) primary

    c) necessary

    d) insignificant

25. The opposite word for nonchalant is:

    a) popular

    b) intelligent

    c) reckless

    d) concerned

26. The same meaning of the word hoax is:

    a) ruse

    b) embargo

    c) crusade

    d) logic

27. Composure also means:

    a) poise

    b) agitation

    c) stimulation

    d) liveliness

28. The opposite word for excise is:

    a) staple

    b) organize

    c) retain

    d) sleep

29. The antonym for the word disperse is:

    a) satisfy

    b) praise

    c) agree

    d) gather

30. The synonym of the word eccentric is:

    a) selective

    b) peculiar

    c) frugal

    d) normal

31. Which of the following is the synonym for the word commendable?

    a) accountable

    b) noticeable

    c) admirable

    d) irresponsible

32. The synonym for domain is:

    a) territory

    b) formation

    c) rebellion

    d) entrance

33. The word that also means passive is:

    a) emotional

    b) woeful

    c) inactive

    d) lively

34. Liberate is the opposite of:

    a) attack

    b) conserve

    c) restrain

    d) ruin

35. The opposite word for faltering is:

    a) reluctant

    b) explanatory

    c) adoring

    d) steady

36. The synonym for vast is:

    a) immense

    b) slight

    c) attentive

    d) steady

37. The synonym for the word comply is:

    a) entertain

    b) obey

    c) subdue

    d) flatter

38. The opposite word for optimum is:

    a) rational

    b) worst

    c) victorious

    d) mediocre

39. Enlighten is the synonym for:

    a) teach

    b) comply

    c) confuse

    d) relocate

40. The antonym for the word tedious is:

    a) alarming

    b) tranquil

    c) stimulating

    d) intemperate

41. Exonerate is the antonym for:

    a) blame

    b) irritate

    c) respect

    d) minimize

42. The opposite word for ephemeral is:

    a) hidden

    b) temporary

    c) enduring

    d) internal

43. The word predecessor DOES NOT mean:

    a) ancestor

    b) descendant

    c) antecedent

    d) successor

44. The synonym for the word refrain is:

    a) persevere

    b) glimpse

    c) secure

    d) desist

45. The antonym for the word affable is:

    a) eager

    b) simple

    c) hollow

    d) disagreeable

46. The word that also means rigorous is:

    a) tolerable

    b) disorderly

    c) demanding

    d) lenient

47. The antonym for orient is:

    a) simplify

    b) deter

    c) arouse

    d) confuse

48. The opposite for the word levitate is:

    a) sink

    b) whisper

    c) undulate

    d) plod

49. Oblivious also means:

a) unaware

b) conscious

c) sinister

d) visible

50. The synonym for the word verify is:

a) unite

b) refute

c) confirm

d) disclose

51. Pacify is the opposite word for:

a) atomize

b) excite

c) dismiss

d) complicate

52. The antonym for the word plausible is:

    a) credible

    b) unbelievable

    c) apologetic

    d) insufficient

53. The opposite for the word avid is:

    a) unkind

    b) equal

    c) unenthusiastic

    d) partial

54. The opposite word for meek is:

    a) polite

    b) forceful

    c) painful

    d) mild

55. The antonym of ambiguous is:

   a) indefinite

   b) equivocal

   c) certain

   d) apathetic

56. The synonym of confer is:

   a) promise

   b) refuse

   c) consult

   d) confide

57. The opposite meaning of eloquent is:

   a) plain

   b) inarticulate

   c) fluent

   d) shabby

58. Deterrent is the opposite of the word:

    a) discomfort

    b) proponent

    c) obstacle

    d) encouragement

59. The antonym of the word impertinent is:

    a) polite

    b) relentless

    c) rude

    d) animated

60. Augment also means:

    a) increase

    b) evaluate

    c) criticize

    d) repeal

61. The antonym for the word ludicrous is:

    a) charitable

    b) reasonable

    c) somber

    d) absurd

62. Archaic is the opposite of the word:

    a) haunted

    b) ancient

    c) modern

    d) tangible

63. Vindictive is the same as the word:

    a) offensive

    b) spiteful

    c) insulting

    d) outrageous

64. The synonym for the word menial is:

   a) rewarding

   b) dangerous

   c) boring

   d) lowly

65. The synonym of the word panacea is:

   a) necessity

   b) cause

   c) result

   d) cure

66. The opposite word for taut is:

   a) vague

   b) rigid

   c) relaxed

   d) neutral

67. The word glib also means:

    a) insincere

    b) dishonest

    c) insulting

    d) angry

68. The word that also means cognizant is:

    a) confused

    b) mystified

    c) educated

    d) conscious

69. The closest word that also means concurrent is:

    a) substantial

    b) apprehensive

    c) simultaneous

    d) incidental

70. Intrepid is the opposite of:

   a) fearful

   b) chivalrous

   c) consistent

   d) belligerent

ANSWER SHEET

SET 1.

Answer Sheet:

1. a	14. a
2. b	15. c
3. b	16. d
4. c	17. c
5. b	18. c
6. a	19. a
7. b	20. b
8. b	21. c
9. c	22. a
10. b	23. b
11. d	24. c
12. b	25. c
13. b	26. b

27. b

28. c

29. a

30. b

SET 2.

Answer Sheet:

1. b

2. c

3. c

4. b

5. a

6. a

7. b

8. b

9. a

10. d

11. b

12. a

13. b

14. b

15. c

SET 3.

Answer Sheet:

1. a

2. a

3. d

4. b

5. c	24. d
6. b	25. a
7. a	26. c
8. a	27. a
9. a	28. d
10. a	29. b
11. a	30. c
12. c	31. a
13. b	32. a
14. d	33. d
15. c	34. c
16. d	35. b
17. a	36. d
18. c	37. a
19. d	38. c
20. a	39. d
21. d	40. d
22. a	41. d
23. b	42. c

43. a	47. a
44. d	48. c
45. a	49. a
46. b	50. b

SET 4.

Answer Sheet:

1. b	12. a
2. d	13. b
3. d	14. c
4. b	15. a
5. c	16. b
6. b	17. c
7. a	18. c
8. c	19. a
9. c	20. d
10. b	21. d
11. d	22. c

23. b

24. a

25. d

26. a

27. a

28. c

29. d

30. b

31. c

32. a

33. c

34. c

35. d

36. a

37. b

38. d

39. a

40. b

41. a

42. c

43. d

44. d

45. d

46. c

47. d

48. a

49. a

50. c

51. b

52. b

53. c

54. b

55. c

56. d

57. b

58. d

59. a

60. a

61. b	66. c
62. c	67. a
63. b	68. d
64. d	69. c
65. d	70. a

Printed in Great Britain
by Amazon